Bud and Max

by Tristan Horrom
illustrated by Laura Logan

Decodable 9

Mc Graw Hill Education

Bothell, WA • Chicago, IL • Columbus, OH • New York, NY

MHEonline.com

Send all inquiries to:
McGraw-Hill Education
8787 Orion Place
Columbus, OH 43240

ISBN: 978-0-02-145232-3
MHID: 0-02-145232-6

Printed in the United States of America.

7 8 9 LCR 25 24 23

Bud and Max pop up!

But the sun is up.

Dig in, Max!
Dig in!

Bud and Max pop up!

But the sun is not up.

Jump on the box, Bud!